NEUROMARKETING: AND ITS RELATIONSHIP WITH THE ADVERTISING TO REACH THE MIND OF THE CONSUMER.

AUTHOR: Harito fito

Content:

Dedication: 5
Introduction.. 6
Objective: 8

Chapter 1: General aspects of neuromarketing:

1-1: History of neuromarketing............... 9
1-2: Birth of neuromarketing............... 10
1-3: Definition neuromarketing 13
1-4: Objectives of the neuromarketing.... 14
1-5: Advantages of neuromarketing 15
1-6: Disadvantages of neuromarketing......16
1-7: Technology that uses neuromarketing...17
1-8: Neuromarketing as an administrative tool... 27
1-9: Types of neuromarketing 30
1-10: Influence of color in advertising…...35
1-11: The meaning of the colors.................37
1-12: Neuromarketing today 40
1-13: Examples of the of neuromarketing...41
1-14: The marketing Neuromarketing 43

Chapter 2: Elements that influence the behavior of the consumer:

2-1- : Consumer Behavior....................46
2-1-1: Types of consumers................. 48
2-2: customer Satisfaction....................48
2-3: Factors of consumer behavior..........50
2-3-1: cultural factor............................51
2-3-2: personal factors.........................53
2-3-3: Social factors............................55
2-3-4: The family................................ 56
2-3-5: psychological factors...................57
2-4: motivation for the consumer.............58
2-5: perception....................................59
2-6: theories of consumer behavior..........60
2-6-1: economic theory........................60
2-6-2: learning Theory.........................60
2-6-3: psychoanalytic Theory.................61
2-6-4: sociological Theory.................... 63

Chapter 3:

3-1: Neuromarketing..........................63
3-2: Advertising................................65
3-3: neuromarketing in the role of advertising..66
3-4: interactive advertising, persuasion, and consumption.....................................67
3-5: functions of advertising...................69
3-5-1: information function....................69
3-5-2: function persuasive.....................69
3-5-3: economic function......................70
3-6: Objectives of advertising................70
3-6-1: general objectives of the advertising..71

3-6-2: specific objectives of advertising.....71

3-7: types of advertising......................72
3-7-1: stimulation of the primary demand...73
3-7-2: stimulation of the demand selective..74
3-7-3: advertising response direct...........74
3-7-4: advertising response delayed......74

3-7-5: advertising business.................74
3-8: types of advertising......................75
3-8-1: the target audience...................75
3-8-2: the types of the demand: primary or selective...........................75
3-8-3: the messages products or institutional................................76
3-9: types of strategies advertising...........77
3-10: promotional strategies..................79
3-11: affiliate marketing......................79
3-12: five eays to turn the advertising persuasion................................81
3-13: the four 'P'...........................85
3-14: advertising on internet 91
3-15: forms of advertising on the internet..92
3-16: social networks on the internet 92
3-17: e-Mail 93
3-18: web analysis...........................94
   Conclusion..............................95

   Bibliography..............................97

   Annexes.................................100

Dedication:

I dedicate this work first of all to God forgive me the life, the strength, wisdom and strength to move forward, and for my family.

INTRODUCTION:

In this seminar we expose in a clear manner the Neuromarketing its definition and its application as an effective tool to determine the interests of the consumer and some factors to know the mind of the consumer.

We will analyze the influence of Neuromarketing through the hype to get to the mind of the consumer, which studies the stimuli that lead the consumer to behave in a certain way before a product or service. Demonstrating the ability to activate the emotions which is a key factor for attract the consumer and to create an emotional link and earn fidelity.

What it does possible companies to enhance the buying decision and improve their results through advertising. In chapter one we develop the general aspects of neuromarketing, the technology as an influence on the neuroscience, and the key points you need to take on account when designing an advertising campaign to reach the mind of the consumer with greater speed and efficiency.

In chapter two describes the behavior of the consumer, which factors influence the consumer to make their purchasing decision, we will see the types of consumers, that is so important to the client involves perception and because. Chapter three describes the advertising and the influence of Neuromarketing, in this point we will see the role of advertising in Neuromarketing, the specific objectives advertising, in the same way as to persuade the mind of the consumer and the types advertising.

OBJECTIVES:

<u>General objective:</u> To analyze the influence of Neuromarketing through advertising to reach the mind of the consumer. <u>Specific objectives:</u> Explain the concepts and overview of neuromarketing to improve the attitude of consumer's purchase. To determine the behavior of consumers through the study of neuromarketing. To express the theory of neuromarketing on role of advertising.

CHAPTIRE 1 :

In this chapter, we mentioned the importance of the process performed by the neuromarketing, concept, stages and the benefits that companies gain from having a good implementation of advertising taking into account the neuroscience, which leads to have a greater vision for the department of sales, the creativity within advertising, including its definition and characteristics.

1. *History of neuromarketing:*

Since its inception, the marketing has been supported in other disciplines to achieve their purposes, disciplines such as sociology, economics, and neuropsychology, occurred an evolution of such a magnitude that resulted in a new creation of discipline known as neuromarketing. This evolution had its beginnings in the early 90's, which was named decade of the brain, it was at this time that the marketing became a tool indispensable for businesses. (Braidot, 2013, page 15) Neuromarketing is a science that began to be used in the 2002 from then began to be popular, perhaps too lightly coming to banalizarse its initial origin and the goal of their research. This discipline encompasses much more to find the perfect color for the new packaging, or where to place the button of purchase of a website, there are certain errors of concepts that are suitable to clarify. (Braidot, 2013, page 15).

1.2 Birth of neuromarketing:

The rise of neuroscience and the birth of neuromarketing in the 1970s with the first studies applied to marketing in the knowledge of the self-human process advertising messages and behaves in commercial contexts with a bet by a sales approach aimed at the masses. And it is from the early 80's when it comes to strategic marketing in which looking at ways of encouraging demand lower than the supply, through the knowledge and the Satisfaction of underlying needs of consumers.

(Zoega, 2015, page 57) In a nutshell a step forward in the marketing thanks to the inclusion research studies of markets and the interest in psychoanalytical techniques with which are detected as tastes, preferences and needs of the consumer.

Neuromarketing is considered to be an experimental science in the application of techniques belonging to the neurosciences in the field of marketing, study the effects of advertising and other communication actions in the human brain in order to be able to predict the behavior of the consumer.

(Zoega, 2016, page 59) It is, therefore, a specialized type of market research that uses the biometric measurement of the brain activity, eye-tracking, the rhythm the heart, or the galvanic skin response of the subjects studied, to obtain results. (Jones and Monieson, 1990), ' say the authors that the start of Neuromarketing such as it is known today in the market research begins in the 80's exponent of the maturity of the market,' out of concern for the customer service, the quality, loyalty and the loyalty of the brands that then would be lost with the crisis economic. (Zoega, Neuromarketing, 2015). Previously, 'marketing focused its activities on the set of the well-known four PS: Product, Price, Distribution, Advertising and Promotion.

A year later in 6 the decade of the 1990s, the concept of four C's was introduced a replacement more oriented to the client with two theories based on similar concepts. Proposes a more oriented from the perspective of the consumer in the integrates the mass marketing focused on the niche market of the client take into account the cost, the value of the expectations, communication, and convenience of the client. (Zoega, Neuromarketing, 2015) New technologies have helped to revitalize the marketing of the past few years, maintaining goals with messages of products on sale with which to reach the customer. A context in which it should be noted that the consumption patterns of the consumers has changed as a result of the current environment. For this reason, now more than ever, it is necessary to employ new techniques and strategies to achieve these specific needs of consumers with customized products and services through neuroscience applied. (Zoega, Neuromarketing, 2015).

Hence, it is necessary to take into account the influence of the environment, to learn how to focus on the relationships in the transaction between the seller and the purchaser, in which there are all kinds of influences such as interdependencies, and interactions reciprocities between the two. The marketing, not only with the traditional features but also with the vision strategic decisions of the company which includes the interest on the market research of marks by the neuromarketing.

(Zoega, Neuromarketing, 2015). Neuromarketing and market research have become in the environment today a growing number of companies and marketing departments, analyze scientifically the identification of critical factors in the quality of service through the implementation of gauges related to neuroscience and marketing.

In this way the technological advances at the service of research of the human being and the consumer market let you know how it reacts to an individual before the stimuli for marketing and to know the level of attention, emotion, pleasure, and memory (recall and recognition), or to feel an experience in order to seduce the consumers. (Zoega, Neuromarketing, 2016).

1.3 Definition of neuromarketing:

Neuromarketing is the application of techniques of neuroscience to the field of marketing, studying the effects of advertising in the human brain with the intention of reaching out to predict the behavior of the consumer, and based on this create optimal strategies. Neuromarketing is the discipline that relates to the marketing and the behavior of the consumer through neuroscience, and applying the results to the strategy of marketing. (Laborda, 2015, page 209) Focused on marketing, and since the boom of growth and positioning in the business world, will be the new trend in market research known as neuromarketing, giving a response to the obtaining of information accurate information about the client, the market and the environment.

To implement real strategies that provide positive results for the organization on issues of earnings and participation; all this, because many studies have shown that the decisions made day-to-day is carried out with the subconscious. (Laborda, 2015, page 209) That assumes, then, what was raised for the methodologies of classical research markets are global in nature, assessing the perceptions of the client's rational and not since its appearance irrational and particular.

Neuromarketing is a new system of research that today is gaining notoriety in a market that continuously incorporates new formulas, techniques and approaches, in order to acquire a position of "top" in the mind of the consumer. (Braidot, 2013, pp. 16,17) Advertisers, in his tireless quest to reach the mind of the consumer and convince them that your product is the best of all, they have not passed the opportunity to employ in his work the new science tools it puts at your scope. Neuroscience is no exception, and the techniques of Neuromarketing are gaining more and more prominence. (Braidot, 2013, pp. 16,17).

1.4 Objectives of neuromarketing:

Learn how the nervous system translates the vast amount of stimuli that the individual receives every day in the language of the brain, and the processing of such stimuli. To study the effectiveness of the advertising messages guide the selection of the format media most appropriate for the emotional connection with the consumer. (Zoega, 2016, p. 89)

a) to Study the mind of the consumer as to predict its future conduct.
b) (b) Develop effectively all aspects of marketing communications, product, pricing, promotions, etc.
c) to Improve the strategic planning of brand or branding: positioning, segmentation, etc, All focused on the real needs, expectations and desires of the consumer. (Zoega, 2016, page 89).

1.5 Advantages of neuromarketing:

1) The neuroscience allows us to know and deepen the scope of which is beyond the consciousness of the individuals, the driving subconscious.

2) to Develop all aspects of marketing: segmentation, positioning, communications, product, brand, price and channels, with a message more in line with what that the person you are going to consume.

3) With Neuromarketing, decreases the risk business because they are made products that are more closely linked with what we really want people.

4) Neuromarketing would lead to improvements in the techniques and the resources, advertisements and help to understand the relationship between the mind and the conduct of the recipient.

5) neuroscience detected the difficulty or inability on the part of the consumers express the emotional reasons that generate their habits of consumption, and their reactions to different stimuli marketing. (Echaberri, 2014, p. 28.29) Research and studies have shown that the decisions of the consumption is based on subjective feelings, and these feelings are linked with sensory stimuli that are activated at the time of consumption. (Echaberri, 2014, page 28.29).

1.6 Disadvantages of neuromarketing:

1) science is not able to advance to the frenetic pace imposed by the marketing: marketing and the science are moved by interests very different, and have a mode proceed diametrically opposite. On the one hand, science is based on rigorous observation and the test error, during a long process of research, where the outcomes are small advances, which are not necessarily generalizable. In other hand, the marketing need specific answers, immediate application key that will ensure an increase in sales. In short, solutions that science is not able to provide with such celerity. (Neuromarketing, 2013, p. 1).

2) neuromarketing is not able to manipulate the mind: the neuromarketing is not able to manipulate the mind, but to interpret it, to know the answers of the human brain, what

stimuli affect and how. Until the moment it is only able to find out if that reaction is positive or negative, but neither measure what sensations it produces. (Neuromarketing, 2013, p. 1).

3) By the time the neuromarketing key does not exist infallible to interpret information. The data have to be interpreted, which makes the introduction of a factor of risk, and the different analysis tools can give you, therefore, different results compared to the same reality. (Neuromarketing, 2013, p. 1).

In the world of neuromarketing is not for the time being very transparent, that there is some misinformation when it comes to analyzing what they do the different suppliers.

1.7 neuromarketing as a powerful tool:

Neuromarketing has been revealed as a powerful tool due to the effects that produces the advertising in the brain, and to what extent it affects the behavior of the potential customers, it has been called neuromarketing.

The main instrument that is used in this discipline are the Images functional magnetic resonance imaging. (White, 2013, p. 9) The scientists were able to establish some facts that of course the advertisers they began to use as possessed in their campaigns. In the first place, it was learned that the decision to buy or not a certain product is not rational, but that derives from forces unconscious. This statement, which may get nervous to more of a reader, he explains, for example; impulse buying. Surely more than once you have arrived home with a product that you know that you will not use it for anything, but that you have not been able to avoid buy.

(White, 2013, p. 9) Neuromarketing has been revealed as a powerful tool for understanding the relationship between the mind and the behavior of the consumer. Scientists have shredded the purchase process, and know perfectly well what zones of your favorite store catches your attention, or how much time it takes each action you carry out during the process of selection and purchase of each kind of shit you have to home. And these data help the geniuses of marketing to organize the distribution of the articles in the local to end up buying far more of the things that you really need to. (Laborda, 2015, page 225) Until the "invention" of neuromarketing, only he couldn't speculate about what was happening in the mind of the customer.

Thousands of good products sank hopelessly in oblivion due to a bad marketing strategy, while other made its manufacturers to re-filthy rich. The amazing thing is that no one could explain for sure why such a thing happened.

But now, the sophisticated techniques of neuromarketing can measure exactly what will happen when a product reaches the market. (Laborda, 2015, page 225).

1.7.1 The influence of advertising in the neuromarketing:

Today, in our society, the massive presence of advertising is something completely normal. People are bombarded by advertising from many forms and at many times being an increasingly intrusive and sometimes little subtle.
 Probably such amount of advertising does not carry out its function and in the end, the desired the object that I wanted to sell, it is on the ledge that was. As they say, what less pleasing and more anger.
 In this sense, it seeks to understand what is what pleasing to people? It is here, where it enters the Neuromarketing. (Clow K. and., page 472).
 All this reality is a reality, artificial, created with a clear goal to which try to bring people down different roads. Paths that are not random, but are marked with great precision, these marks are the result of the market research which can extract the information needed to create that type of stimuli, pretending to influence the conduct.
 Stimuli of which none is libra.

Thanks to the knowledge of neuromarketing, advertising focuses more on the points that should be exploited as, for example, the emotions, or even all the senses that may be, we have already seen as in the large supermarkets are stimulated senses by means of the music. (Kennethe, p. 472)

But not only that, but there are also other types of experiential marketing that they are being exploited in the same way that music.

Who has not entered into a shop with a characteristic odor that can perfectly be associated with the product sold? The large amount of data that provides the neuroscience on the stimuli to which we react, you should not turn away from the whole idea in the neuromarketing is used as one more tool in the marketing so that in the end the strategy created for the marketing consulting services takes us on the right path to get the target sale. (Kennethe, p. 472) Of note is that with such a great amount of information strategy intended, it will be a lot more appropriate and with the actions so finely tuned that will be most appropriate, within the same strategy.

1.7.2 Technology that uses neuromarketing:

The technology is one of the fundamental tools that complement the neuromarketing already in charge of the study of the processes of the brain of the people and the changes that this is taking on when these decisions, with the purpose of to predict the behavior that this is going to have, so they can study the areas of the brain that is activated when the customer decides between one brand or another.

The use that is given is in the area of marketing, for example in the area of market research, in the research of the behavior of the client, in the validation of the television commercial, design of new products and the impact advertising. (Ramos, 2015, page 303).

1.7.2.1 Technology that uses neuromarketing:

Some of the technologies that Neuromarketing uses are: Functional magnetic resonance imaging: This is responsible for monitoring the physiological functions, is one of the best generates results very complete and reliable, but it is very expensive.

Electroencephalography: Who is in charge of the measurement of the electrical changes that you have the brain, this it is the cheapest of all, it can be seen in *figure 1.*

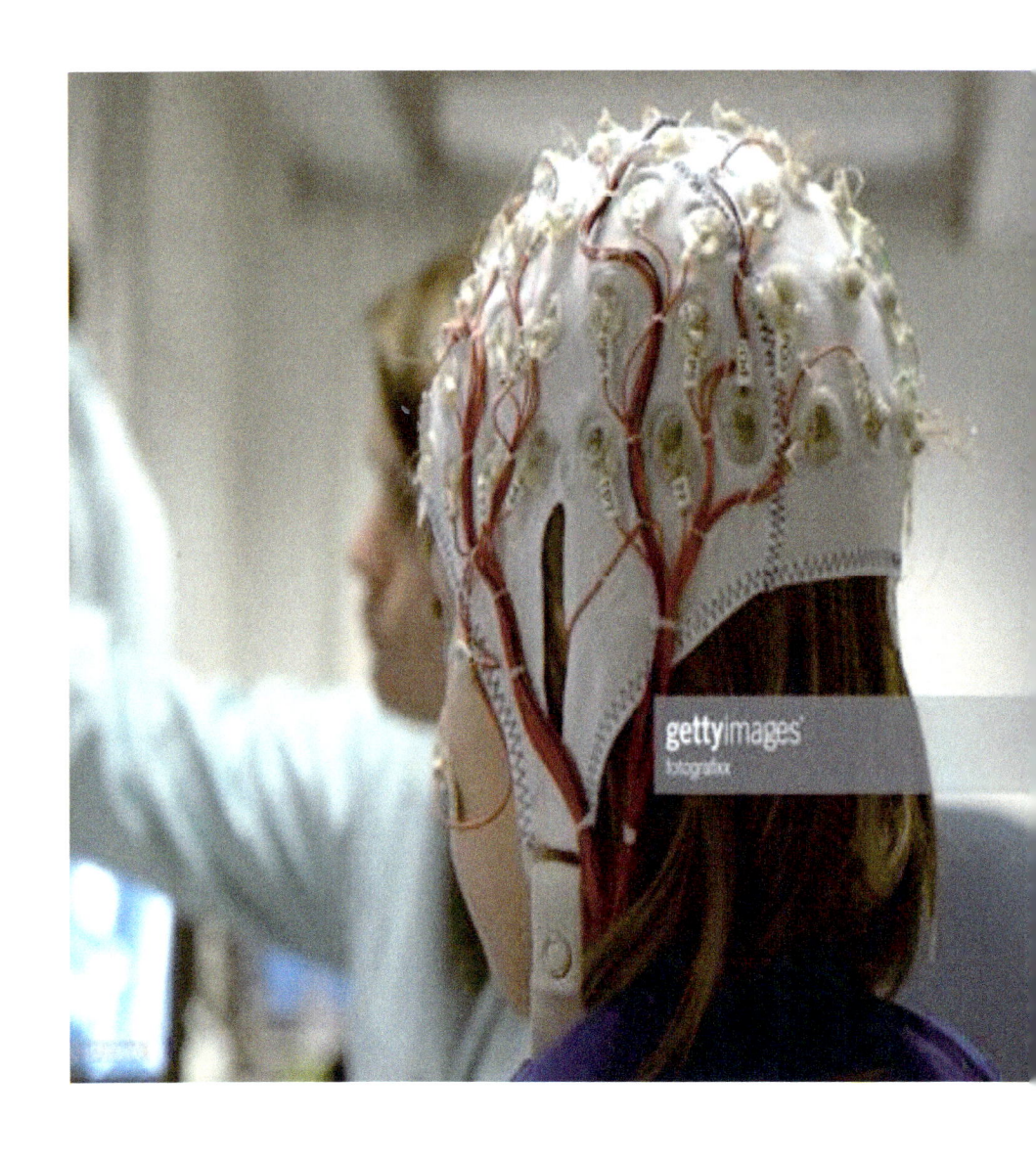

Figure 1: electroencephalography (neuromarketing, 2019)

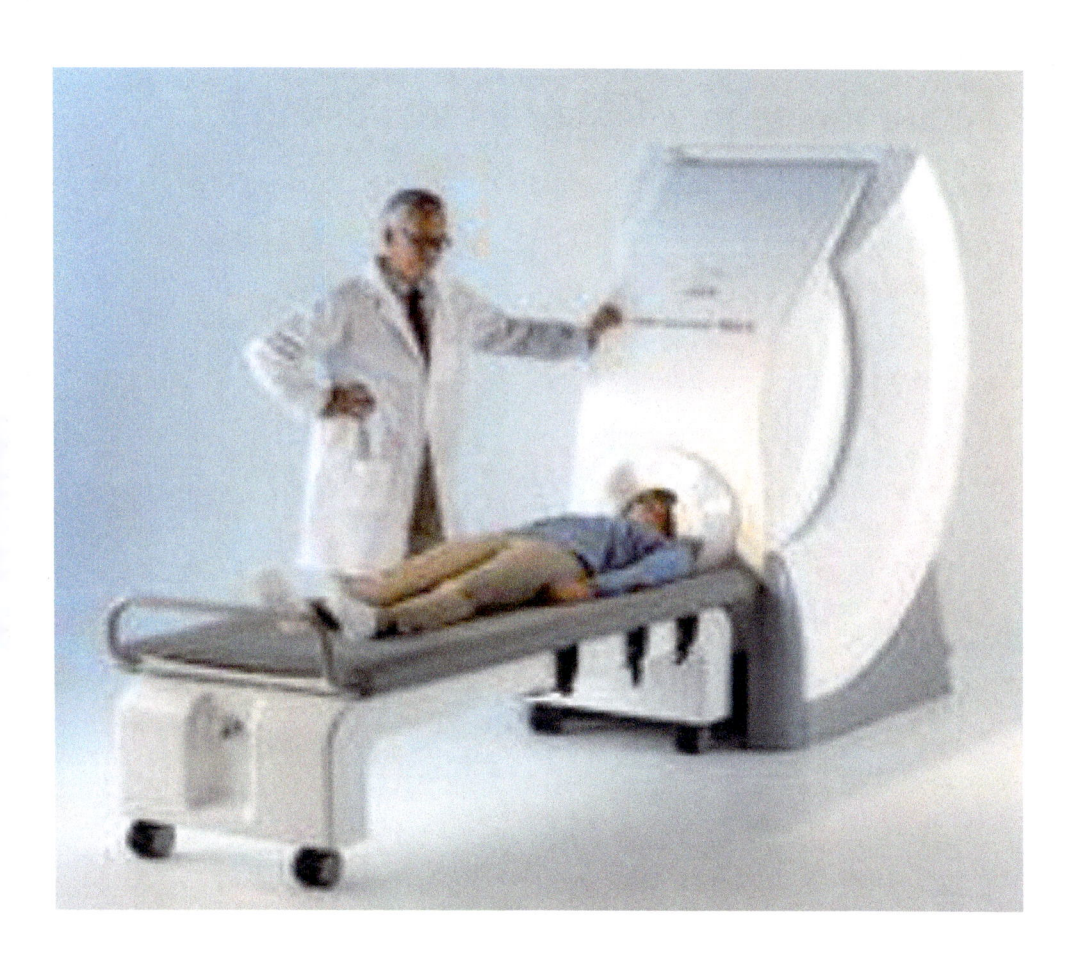

Magneto-Electroencephalography: This measures the magnetic changes that are produced in the brain.

Figure 2: magneto-electroencephalography (Neuromarketing, 2019)

Monitors the physiological functions that may be altered with the activity the brain is an example of this is the metabolism.

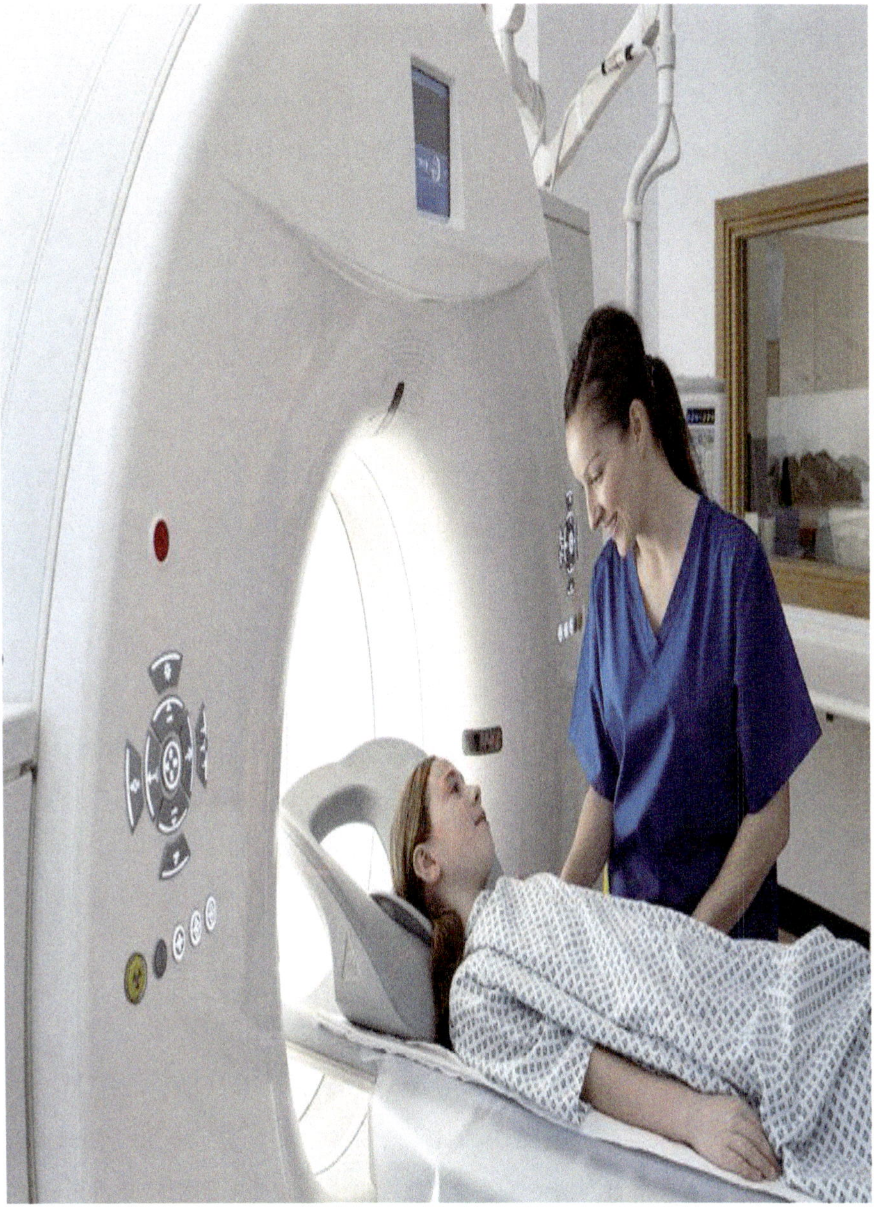

Figure 3. Magnet tomography (neuromarketing, 2019)

All of these technologies were created with the purpose of measuring waves brain, taking into account 3 features;

a) The first is the attention this is achieved more easily in an ad.

(b) The second is the emotion that has to be going up and down as if it is very high cause exhaustion and if it is too low you lose the emotion of the customer.

c) And finally, the memory that is the most difficult to achieve because you have to make a good advertisement for the person to remember, after you have seen. (White, Neuromarketing, p. 9).

1.8 Neuromarketing as an administrative tool:

The growth of neuromarketing as a mechanism to expand the understanding of the customer or consumer, as well as their application is still recent and limited, due to the various factors among which there are few companies that provide associated services with this field. (Kanuk, 2010, p. 2)

1. Companies that increased demand services and implement neuromarketing as a key tool to position itself in the market are big companies, as they have the necessary resources and coverage for reach the masses.

2. The conception entrepreneurs and business sectors based on my smes, do not have clarity about the knowledge and use of this field for their organizations, which generates false exceptivas in front of their scope and impact in the market. (Kanuk, 2010).

3. Companies providing services in neuromarketing not only are devoted to to support this type of alternative practices, if not also traditional practices of the marketing with the aim of gradually introducing their portfolio companies in various events such as conferences, among others.

   They see an opportunity to refocus their business models from go beyond what you apparently want the consumer and the way that they have played to achieve retain its market. (Kanuk, 2010, p. 3).

    4. Neuromarketing is still in an initial state of development, because, the not to be crowded their basis or their applicability discussed in the field business and academic. The findings and

conclusions surrounding this field are not significant for most of stakeholders in the search for alternatives to understand the consumer and provide value through a successful experience in connection with your product or service of your preference. (Kanuk, 2010, p. 3)

4. The managers of the market area of the large companies have a wider knowledge of the advantages of neuromarketing that allow them to implement changes competitive to achieve a key position for their companies in the market.

In contrast, managers of marketing of smes do not have a clarity with in this regard, which implies that the training of your staff, processes, strategies, objectives and business practices are not adapted to the requirements of the market and consumer current due to a short-term vision or limited in their business models. (Kanuk, 2010) The reason why the leaders of the organizations, and the departments of marketing must to take on the challenge of having criteria of academic training and high in your respective field of action; that enable them to understand the dynamics of the market national and international and introduce new ways to innovate your vision and practices business in order to be more competitive.

The techniques and technologies with traditional marketing is no longer sufficient to uncover the true intentions of the consumers, which is why the neuromarketing is displayed as a tool for business flexible and dynamic to create a relationship lasting in the minds of these. Through the implementation of new practices that allow them to improve their ability to create messages, marks, products, services, promotions, among others; designed to achieve a loyalty markets compliance, educating and serving the desires, needs and expectations of consumers. (Kanuk, 2010) Likewise, a challenge to the institutions of control of the markets, implies a profound research, renewal and creation of regulatory mechanisms that allow the consumers be protected from the abuses of the companies that are not ethics used neuromarketing to achieve their goals business. Similarly, the organizations should implement a code of ethics that allow give an image a transparent and responsible for this kind of alternative mechanisms in the various sectors where it has applicability. (Kanuk, 2010).

1.9 Types of neuromarketing:

There are three types of Neuromarketing visual, auditory and kinesthetic, the three are different from each other.

1.9.1 Visual;

It is based on the sense of sight and how we perceive things through our eyes. It is shown that the images come much more quickly to the brain, and the message that you want to be transmitted are received with much more effectiveness. Before the digital era, the standard more valued in advertising were the commercials in visual media, billboards, etc.

Figure 4: Neuromarketing Visual. (Neuromarketing, 2019)

1.9.2 Ear;

Focuses on the basis of what we hear, and as is generated by means of the ear a perception of the world. There's a type of people who are more sensitive to the music, sounds and silences in the process of communication. They are an example of the spots where it is given more rope to the music or sounds by part of the features of the same product. The ear has properly fibers nerve and is able to distinguish close to different frequencies. (Cayuela, p. 171) To others to hear and listen, this body allows you to be aware of our position in the space and our movements, to control the sense of balance and perform coordinated movements, recognize people and objects that are outside of your field visual and building a store of memories. Auditory memory is a brain process dynamic and active encoding and stores the information that is linked to the present experiences and knowledge above the sounds. (Cayuela, p. 171) In the Neuromarketing music, whose peculiarities are found in different parts of the brain, is a means of communication with the customer. Like the visual, the hearing is global rather than analytical, this causes us to obtain a sound image complete with images, melody, rhythm, timbre and intensity.

Figure 5. Neuromarketing hearing. (Neuromarketing, 2019)

1.9.3 Kinesthetic:

It is considered, not the least important to the above, it is used less often because it is through touch, taste, and smell. The standard in which it is presented is when certain points of sale are performed tastings and presentations products and people can taste, touch, and depends on the product, smell it. The touch is more used by the female gender as it goes more with the language communication of this genre.

On the other hand, the sense of taste are related to and mix with the others as the thermal sensations, tactile, and olfactory. (Cayuela, pp. 193, 201, 213) The brain works along with the tongue to taste food, to recognize a flavor the brain needs information that you receive the nose and the tongue for different nerves. Each q we see an announcement second by second, plane by plane.

This mode is they can make decisions as, for example, to withdraw a given plane of the final announcement or add an additional sequence, can also be measured many other concepts, as the activation of the subject or the subject's emotional state when you receive the product in screen. (Cayuela, pp. 193, 201, 213).

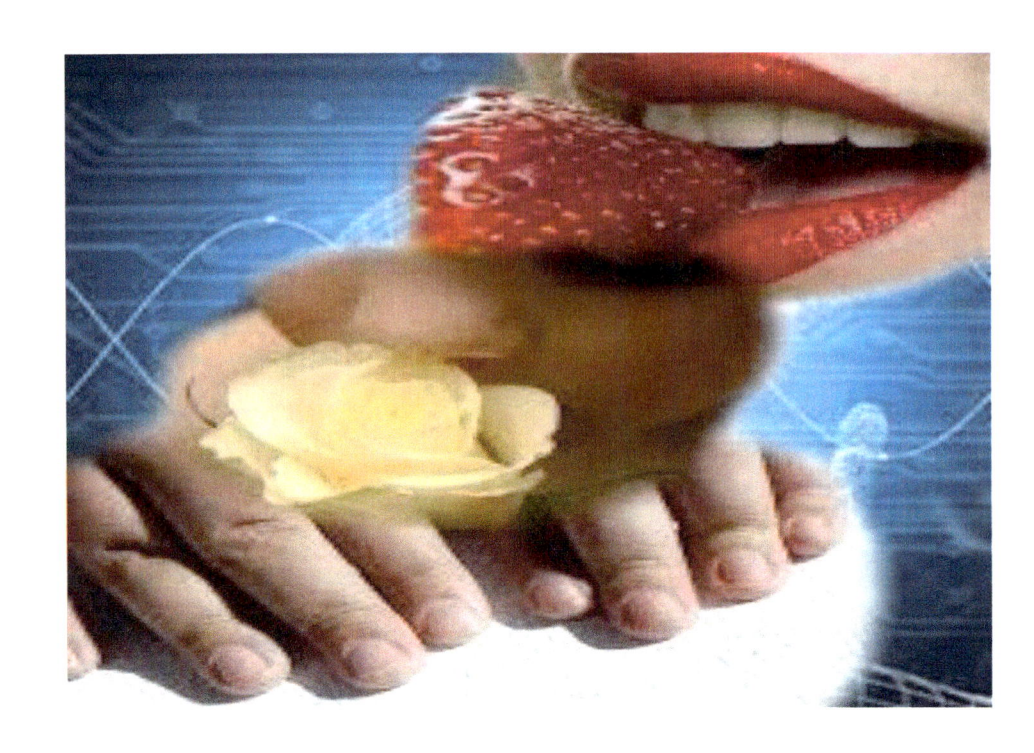

Figure 6 Neuromarketing kinesthetic (neuromarketing, 2019)

1.10 Influence of color in advertising:

There are many factors that influence what and how to buy consumers. No however, a large part of these decisions are influences by means of signals visual, being the color the stronger and more persuasive. When you promote new products, it is crucial to keep in mind that the consumers position the visual appearance and color above other factors such as sound, smell and texture.

In this way, the brands develop their strategies based on the conquest emotional and senses to get your product and/or service is the chosen one for consumers and gain the loyalty of its customers for the longest time possible, using tools such as those provided by the neuromarketing to know the tastes of your potential customers. (Cremades, 2014, p. 303)

While always knew that there are brands that have a unique impact level emotional, the great novelty that brings neuromarketing is that today you can explore in "how" and "why" of the election of the customer, in advance, and reliable. This opens a field of unprecedented possibilities for companies wishing to work with the objective of owning a place in the market that guarantee success the present and the future. Why certainly, the perception of color by part of the man has a psychological determinant. (Cremades, 2014, p. 303) Color influences our mood, our temper in general, though not all react to the stimulus of a color in the same way. Regardless of the context in space and time and, above all, the perspective in to observe an object, the reaction to this stimulus is determined by other factors such as the idiosyncrasies of society, the culture, the religion, the context historical occurs, the circumstances, etc Psychologists have found that a simple look at different colors we alter the blood pressure, heart beat and the rhythm of the breath, as you hear a jarring sound or chord musical harmonious.

The vivid colors that cancel each other out, as loud sounds or voices high, you can reach us no harm the eye or give us a headache; the soft colors and harmonious, such as music and gentle voices, we're thrilled, or we sosiegan. Although often the color is indicative of a state of mind, it is not always infallible. (Cremades, 2014).

1.11 the meaning of the colors:

Studies have shown that each color has influence psychologically on the people at the to make a purchase, 85% of consumers is guided mainly by him at the decide to put in the cart or not a product. Each advertising campaign is designed strategically to impact the target market through the color that appeals to you more, depending on the sex, age, level socio-economic or even geographical area. (Cremades, 2014) Market researchers have been able to verify that the color affects well the buying habits of people. For example, people impulsive are guided by the red, blue, or black, while the buyers that plan their expenditures are guided by the pink and the light colors. But what are the colors that most influence the advertising? To know what color works in your campaign or business, you should establish strategies, objectives, purposes and to develop concepts according to your market. The visual identity is one of the most important factors for success. (Cremades, 2014).

  (a) Red: It is a color that represents power, attraction, and manages to keep the attention of the consumer. Color is sensual and seductive; it is the most used in the marketing. Draws the attention and stimulates the mind. It is used in products consumption as a beverage and fast-food restaurants.

  (b) Blue: It is a color that conveys a calm, confident and relaxed. It is identified by be the color of the sky and the water, that makes it more familiar. In dark tones represents elegance and success, and in clear tones freshness and youth. Used in technological products or personal hygiene.

(c) Green: It is a color that refers to the nature and stream ecological values. It is a color that is used for the care of the health and good intentions. It is versatile, pleasant and with a wave. It is a color that is usually always works without error.

 d) Yellow: It is a color risky, bold and brilliant. Captures easily care of the children's market, more in boys than girls, but conveys happiness and a lot of light. It is a color that makes it stand out from the crowd.

(e) Orange: Color is considered as energy, is used for the promotion of sports products, energy drinks and vitamins.

It is a color that always motivates innovation and youth. A problem with this color, it is that businesses classical used to give impressions incorrect, missing out on occasions credibility.

f) Purple: The color is considered as royalty, mystery and spirituality. It is a feminine color, elegant and at the same time cold and warm. Used to promote products of fantasies and inspire you to overcome.

g) Pink: It is a color associated with childhood, femininity and innocence. Draws mostly girls and girls because it is a bright color, lively and alive. It is a color that is used in women to attract men, used by both in the last few years. It is usually used in brands of toys, and make-up detergents.

h) Brown: Is the color that represents the earth, and wood. Transmitted simplicity and warmth. It is considered by many as the less color eye-catching, but many brands use packaging of cafes, food, organic or fine chocolates.

(i) White: universal Color that symbolizes peace and purity, is often used in funds or in negative space of the design. Many products come to the white to appear cleanliness and clarity. In the published is seen in campaigns minimalist generally or completely new products.

j) Black: it Is considered as a color elegant and simple. It is the most versatile all and goes with everything. It is used by companies both traditional and modern. Conveys drama and fear. Usually seen in campaigns fashion.

1.12 Neuromarketing today:

1. Brain Neocortex: The brain is logical and rational. Although many of the decisions are taken unconsciously, this brain is in charge of explaining the decisions from the logical conscious. (Braidot, 2013, page 24)
2. Limbic Brain: It is the brain that stores feelings and emotions and tends to be more important than the Neocortex at the time of decision making. (Braidot, 2013, page 24)
3. Reptilian Brain: Also called the reptilian is the brain that deals with the feelings of survival of human being as they are playing, domination, defense, fear, protection, etc (Braidot, 2013, page 23) Neuromarketing evaluates the brain when it is exposed to a message, and measured three components: attention, emotion and memory.
 1) attention it is easy to capture in an advertisement, which causes often have a high value.

2) The emotion should go up and down during the announcement, as if the emotion is very high for a long time can lead to fatigue and decrease significantly the effectiveness of the ad.

3) memory is the most difficult thing to achieve. The brand it should show up in the moments the announcement that most captures the attention of the consumer for the brand remember at the end of the announcement. It is important to note that to remember an ad does not it means that you are going to buy the product.

1.13 Examples of the use of neuromarketing: *Challenge Pepsi*

A test of Neuromarketing very documented on the Internet is called the challenge Pepsi that consisted in giving a test to a group of people of two drinks that were not visual difference. The result surprised as more than 50% of the people chose Pepsi versus Coca Cola, when Pepsi had approximately 25% of the market queues.

The test is repeated on another group of people, but this time seeing the marks, visualizing the activity of their brains via magnetic resonance imaging. The area responsible for the positive reward of the brain was activated with both soft drinks, without however, it was identified that activated another extra area of the brain to know the brand. This last test if agreed as a result, the share of the market since the 75% of the respondents chose Coca-Cola. (Challenge Pepsi) With these two studies concluded that the sale of Pepsi should be at the moment the study, slightly more than 50% of the market, however, both the actual values of the market as the brain's response to know the brands was far superior to please Coca Cola compared to Pepsi.

Until recently, it was very difficult to examine the brain mechanisms that put into operation the memories, feelings, emotions, learning and the perceptions that determine the behavior of the consumer. (Challenge Pepsi) Now, research from the neurosciences is registering a great advance for helping us to understand and improve the processes of decision decisions, as well as the behavior of people in front of the consumption of goods and services. (Challenge Pepsi) The aim is to understand how the sensory systems of the brain encode the information from the outside world, that is to say, how does the nervous system to translate the huge number of stimuli to which it is exposed an individual to the language in the brain: activation and deactivation of neurons, communication between neurons, transmit information and the phenomena of neuro-plasticity.

This is, without a doubt, a quantum leap that began to take shape during the years ninety and led to the development of techniques of analysis of images (which evolve, also, at an amazing rate). This evolution is allowing it to not only confirm empirically a set of assumptions of traditional marketing, but also have access to a field of knowledge of the enormous possibilities of the application in the organizational management. (Challenge Pepsi).

1.14 The marketing Neuromarketing:

Since its inception, the activity of marketing is based on knowledge from other disciplines, such as psychology, sociology, the economy, the exact sciences, and anthropology. Upon joining the advances of neuroscience and neuropsychology, there was an evolution of such a magnitude that resulted in the creation of a new discipline, that we know with the name of neuromarketing. (White, 2013) This evolution brought with it the development of a set of methodologies which application shone a light on issues where we've been in the dark for years, and it is estimated that in the Twenty-first Century will yield huge advances in knowledge about the functioning of the brain.

Which, in turn, the development of novel methodologies to investigate and explain the key processes of decision making in front of the consumption of products and services and, at the same time, to create and implement strategic plans that lead to successful organizations toward their goals. (White, 2013) Without a doubt, the neuromarketing brings with it a set of resources of enormous value to investigate the market, segmental and develop successful strategies in the field of products (design, brand, packaging, positioning, pricing, communications, and channels.

The methodologies used by the neuromarketing are varied and come in the most of the field of neuroscience. (White, 2013) The neuroimaging techniques allow you to investigate what is going on in the brain of a client with the different stimuli that it receives, which provides a field of study much more potent than that provided by the traditional marketing due to their limitations for to explore the mechanisms' goal aware of, that are determined by more than 90% of the decisions of the customers. For example: When using the functional magnetic resonance imaging, each exploration let's see how and where it triggers the brain to each stimulus while they are working. Imagine the reader the scope of this methodology because, according to the areas of the brain that triggered, we can investigate (among many other aspects): What are the attributes of a product or service that generate acceptance, rejection or indifference.

This can be done with knowledge of brand and test blind, such as he did Read Montagne in the United States with Coca-Cola and Pepsi. (Challenge Pepsi) The level of acceptance (pre-test) and remembrance (post-test) of a commercial, in any of its formats: television, radio, graphics, public roads, etc., and the degree of impact of each one of its parts, both in the aspects neurosensory as in the concerning the mechanisms of attention, emotion and memory.

The strength of the attachments emotional to a particular brand. (White, 2013) The stimuli that must be implemented in a point-of-sale to encourage the shopping. This list can be as extensive as required by the marketing management. In the currently, most of the studies with neuroimaging techniques are carried out in institutes specialized (the most advanced countries are the United States and Germany) and their results are very useful for the companies which want to make use of them.

Without a doubt, the increasing development of devices that explore and, above all, located the brain activations has opened up a field of studies truly exciting, with results that leave behind many assumptions of the past. (White, 2013).

Chapter two: **Elements that influence the behavior of the consumer**

In this chapter, we will establish the dynamics and introduction to the study of behavior of the consumer and their evolution, and examines how the fact of providing value is the basis for create and retain satisfied customers and profitable, and described the great influence of new technologies and the new media of communication in the study of the consumers through the study of the mind of this. Reference is made about the relationship between the principles of the behavior of a consumer study to get to capture their attention. By using a perspective wide about the process and the techniques used to study patterns of consumption.

2.1 consumer Behavior:

Defines consumer behavior as the behavior exhibited by the the finding, purchasing, using, evaluating and disposing of products and services that they expect to meet their needs. Consumer behavior focuses on the manner in which consumers and families or households make decisions to spend their available resources (time, money, effort) in articles related to the consumption. That includes what they buy, why they buy, when, where, how often what they buy, how often to use it, how they evaluate it after the purchase, the effect of such evaluations on future purchases, and how disposed of. (Kanunk, 2010, page 309)

While all consumers are unique, one of the constants most important among all, despite the differences, is that they are all consumers. Usually it is used or consume food, clothing, shelter, transportation, education, computer, holiday, needs, luxuries, services and even ideas. (Kanunk, 2010, page 309) Consumers play a vital role in the health of economies, local, national and international. The purchase decisions we make affect the demand for basic raw materials to transportation, manufacturing, banking influence the employment of workers and deployment of resources, the success of some industries and the failure of others.

To be successful in any business, and especially in the dynamic market and rapidly evolving present, the mercadólogos have to know how much they can about consumers: what they want, what they think, how they work and how to use your free time. (Kanunk, 2010, page 309) Need to understand the influences of personal and group affect the decisions of consumers and the way in which to make such decisions. And, in these days in which the media options are on the rise, not only do they need

identify your target audience, but you also need to know where and how to get to him.
In its broadest sense, the behavior of the consumer describes two types different entities of consumption. (Kanunk, 2010, page 309).

2.1.1 Types of consumers:

The consumer personal: Purchase goods and services for their own use, for the use of the home, or as a gift to a third party. In each of these contexts, the products are bought for final use of the individuals, to whom we will refer to as end users or final consumers.

(Kanunk, 2010, page 311) The second category of consumers. The consumer organisational: Includes business with for-profit and not-for-profit, to government agencies (local, state, and national), as well as the institutions (e.g., schools, hospitals and prisons), which should buy products, equipment and services for their organizations work.

Despite the importance of both categories of consumers, individuals and organizations. (Kanunk, 2010, page 311).

2.2 customer Satisfaction:

It is the perception in the individual consumer about the performance of the product or service in relation to their own expectations.

As noted, before, the customers they will have expectations to be significantly different. The concept of customer satisfaction is a function of the expectations of the customers. A customer whose experience is less than their expectations (say, a letter wine limited in a restaurant is expensive or cold chips served in a McDonald s) will be dissatisfied. (Schiffman, 2005, page 41) Guests whose experiences meet their expectations will be satisfied.

And customers whose expectations are exceeded (for example, small samples of delicious food "by the chef served between the plates in the restaurant expensive, or a play area for kids, well-designed in a establishment McDonald's) will be very satisfied or even delighted. (Schiffman, 2005, page 41) In effect, both the customer satisfaction as the fact enchants the client have a lot to do with the underlying principles of the marketing concept, and, therefore, strategies are valuable to the marketers should take advantage of. In terms of consumer satisfaction, a study widely cited, where related levels of customer satisfaction with the behavior of the latter, identified various types of customers. (Diaz, 2012, page 321) On the positive side, the customers are completely satisfied, they are loyal and continue to buy, or are apostles whose experiences exceed their expectations and make very positive comments from person-to-person about the company. In contrast, in the negative side are the deserters, those who feel neutral or fairly satisfied and, in the same way, they could stop doing business with the company; consumers terrorists, who have had negative experiences with the company and disseminated negative comments; and the captives or hostages, who are customers poor unfortunate men who stay with the company because there is an environment of monopolistic or low prices and with whom it is very expensive to treat because complaints continued. (Diaz, 2012, page 41) Finally, there are the mercenaries, even when they are the customers satisfied, in they don't really have an allegiance to the company and may defect in any time, for a lower price elsewhere, or by mere impulse, thus challenging the relationship satisfaction-loyalty.

The researchers propose that companies should strive to create apostles, increase the satisfaction of the deserters and convert them into loyal customers, to avoid having terrorists or captives, and to reduce the number of mercenaries. (Kanunk, 2010, p. 401).

2.3 Factors of consumer behavior:

Marketers point to the consumer as a key piece for businesses, it is also considered as the source of the income of a company. The term consumer behavior is defined as behavior that consumers show when you search, buy, use, evaluate, and dispose of products and services that will meet your needs. Consumer behavior focuses on how individuals make decisions to spend their available resources and the factors that influence these decisions.

The factors that most influence the purchase decisions of the consumers: cultural, social, personal and psychological. (Diaz, 2012, p. 330).

2.3.1 cultural Factor:

The culture, subcultures and social classes are a major factor in the consumer behavior. Culture is the determinant of the desires and behavior of people. The children, as they grow, they acquire a set of values, perceptions, preferences and behaviors of their family and a number of other key institutions.

Each culture is formed by subcultures smaller they provide to their members factors of identification and socialization more specific. (Diaz, 2012, page 332) At present, companies have developed technologies of information and communication that allow transmission of information and interactions, not only between the members of a given community, but between isolated communities until a few years ago.

This leads us to ask ourselves if we really are dealing with a 28 single macro in western culture, globalized and uniform or, on the contrary, each community is keeping cultural differences are relevant. (Diaz, 2012, page 332) Therefore, if we assume as a starting point idea of cultural variety in the world, is apparent that the consumer is no stranger to this influence, so that delimit which are the cultural aspects that most influence is at all relevant. In a few words you could define the cultural factor such as: what defines and characterizes a society, the set of values, traditions, and customs that are shared. Subcultures include nationalities, religions, racial groups and areas geographical. When subcultures are segments of extensive markets and influential, companies tend to design marketing programs special.

(Diaz, 2012, page 332) These aspects of uniqueness sometimes have important implications in the knowledge of the consumer and in developing good marketing strategies. Is pay special attention to the subcultures that are distinguished by their age and their ethnic characteristics. (Diaz, 2012, page 332) Social classes have a number of characteristics: Tend to behave in a similar way to the ones that belong to social classes different. They differ in the way they dress, talk, in the preferences entertainment and many other factors. Second, the people occupy positions higher or lower depending on the class to which they belong. Finally, the social class of a person is determined by a number of variables as their profession, their income, their welfare, their education and their values, and not so much by a single variable.

Also, people can change social class throughout your life. The degree of mobility will vary according to the rigidity of social stratification of each society. (Diaz, 2012, page 332).

2.3.2 personal Factors:

This factor includes the self-image, health, beauty and fitness. When perceives the product or service as a means to improve the self-image, it becomes stronger and is likely to become more of a factor, durable, and works as a stable trait. Diaz, 2012, page 335)

a) Age and life cycle stage In this factor analyzes the cycle of life that people go through, and their different stages of life, they acquire goods and services that go according to each stage; and as changing tastes depending on the age also expressed in their attitudes, interests and opinions...

(Diaz, 2012, page 335)

(b) life Style: The life style of a person is expressed in their attitudes, interests and opinions, it is something more than social class or personality; outlines a pattern of action and interaction with the world, denoted by full-the person in interaction with his environment. Knowing the life style of a group of people, marketers may lead the brand of your product with greater clarity to this lifestyle and have a greater success in its launch and acceptance of the product. If it is used properly this concept, the marketers will come to understand the changing values of consumer and to know its influence on the buying behavior. (Diaz, 2012, p. 335)

c) Personality and self-concept: It define the personality as psychological characteristics and distinctive of a person as self-confidence, authority, autonomy, sociability, aggressiveness, emotional stability that led to answers to their environment relatively consistent and permanent. Personality influences on the buying behavior of people. The brands also they have personality, and thus, consumers tend to choose brands whose personality is more akin to yours. The brand personality is the set of human traits concrete that could be attributed to a particular brand. (Diaz, 2012, p. 335) Consumers "self-controlled" (sensitive to the idea of how others see him), prefer brands which match best with the situation of consumption. Usually choose and use brands that have a brand personality consistent with their real concept of themselves, although in some cases the choice is based on the concept of ideal selfsame or even in the concept that others have of them, more than a real concept. In conclusion, companies should also consider the events critical or life transitions, such as marriage, the birth of a child, an illness, a move, a divorce, a job change, or widowhood, since these events, awaken new needs. (Diaz, 2012, page 335).

2.3.3 social Factors:

People acquire from their parents a religious orientation, political and economic, and a sense of personal ambition, self-worth, and love. They belong to two Groups of Reference one is made up of all the groups that have an influence, direct (face-to-face) as the family, the friends, the neighbors and the coworkers are all individuals with which people interact constant and informal or indirect about their attitudes or behavior. (Salomon, 2010, page 592).

The second group is a part of secondary groups, such as religious, professional, trade union, which are more formal and require a lower frequency of interaction. Influence people to at least three different ways. In the first place, expose the individual to new behaviors and lifestyles. They also influence their attitudes and the concept they have of themselves.

Finally, the reference groups created pressures which may influence the choice of products and brands. People are also influenced by groups to those who do not belong to, and groups dissociative are those whose values or behaviors rejects the person. (Salomon, 2010, page 592).

2.3.4 The family :

Is the organization buys the most important consumer markets, and their members constitute the reference group is the most influential. Manufacturers products and brands that play in places where the influence group is strong must determine how to reach the opinion leaders of these groups reference and influence them. (Salomon, 2010, page 300).

An opinion leader is a person that moves in circles informal and geared or advice on a product or a category of products determined, opining on what brand is best or how to use a particular product. Companies try to reach opinion leaders by identifying the demographic and psychographic linked to the leadership of opinion, given what means of communication used by the leaders, and speak messages. (Salomon, 2010, page 300).

2.3.5 psychological Factors:

The study of consumer behavior has always been an object of reflection; not however, their methodology has changed to a foundation that is more scientific with the to improve marketing decisions for the process of communication with the same. (Salomon, 2010) Here the role of psychology is basically to discover the relationships of these before the strategies of the market is facing to the proposal of a society as dynamic and constantly changing, as is our that gives rise to a series of new needs that individuals manifest and that arise from the interaction with the environment.

(Salomon, 2010) According to the behaviorist theory of John B. Watson, which was the first one used by the advertisers is to make consumers into believing they need such a product until you feel the need to do this, assume for example that a company of soft drinks you want to sell your product using as a strategy for advertising the idea that quenches your thirst.

Through an incessant bombardment through all means of communication possible, is repeated again and again the same idea to the product "X" calm the thirst in such a way the consumer starts to feel such a need to satisfy a thirst that was caused. Within this factor, we find a series that increasingly the development of strategies of markets. (Salomon, 2010).

2.4 motivation of the consumer:

Stop the psychology of motivation is a set of factors that drive the behavior of human beings to the attainment of an object. For example, a person has many needs at any time. Some are the result of physiological states of tension such as hunger, thirst and the discomfort. Other, the result of the psychological states of tension such as the need for recognition, estimation, or membership. (Diaz, 2012, page 336) In regard to the theory of Maslow, it seeks to explain why certain needs drive the human being at a particular time. For this author, the answer is that human needs are arranged in a hierarchy, from the most urgent to least urgent. (Diaz, 2012, page 336). In order of importance, Maslow hierarchized the needs into physiological, of safety, social, esteem and self-actualization. According to this theory, individuals try to first satisfy the most important needs. (Diaz, 2012, page 336)

When individuals are successful in satisfying an important need, it ceases to be a motivator for a moment, and the person, therefore, will motivated to meet the need that occupies the next place of importance.

2.5 perception:

It is the way in which we apprehend the world around us, people act and react on the basis of their perceptions of reality and not on the basis of a reality objective. It distinguishes the feeling for its active nature as the action perceptive includes an elaboration of the sensory data by the part of the individual. The perception also relates to the external objects, and is made in the level mental, while the feeling is a subjective experience directly derived of the senses. (Diaz, 2012, page 338)

It should be noted that the perception depends not only on the nature of the physical stimuli, but also the relationship between them and the environment, as well as of the conditions of each individual. Human beings may have different perceptions of the same stimulus because the following processes perception: selective Exposure, Distortion, and selective retention. (Diaz, 2012, page 338) That force marketers to work harder to communicate their messages, this explains why it is used so much repetition and scenes shocking to send messages to consumers. (Diaz, 2012, page 338)

To conclude, the reality is that as consumers, we must accept that our behavior is much more complex than we think, and that this is the the result of a large number of psychological factors that are in constant motion for each one of our purchasing processes and are the we will greatly help the sale is successful. (Diaz, 2012, page 338) It becomes essential to know the elementary concepts of psychology shopping enables us to access to a better mastery of the sales in the efforts day-to-day; but, without a doubt, the most important was the finding that the "Psychology of the Sales" is the secret to success. To understand how people think, why they buy and what creative techniques can be used to act, and encourage the individual to finalize the purchase. (Diaz, 2012, page 338).

2.6 Theories of consumer behavior:

2.6.1 economic Theory:

The basis of this theory, one of whose exponents more relevant, is that the man always seeking to maximize their utility. That is to say, the man will always try to achieve the product that is most useful to give in function of the price you will pay for it, in other words, the man will always try to maximize the cost-benefit ratio in every activity of your life. (Consumer, 2007, p. 387).

2.6.2 learning Theory :

In economic theory the purchase of a shampoo must be done by the observation of all the features of all the champ uses existing in the market (or in store). So, after having weighed the pros and cons of all of them (amount, price, additives, perfume, external characteristics, etc.), the client should decide to purchase the one that offers the best overall result. The analysis of the actual behavior shows, however, that in practice it does not it always happens as well, but normally people buy only those products who knows and who previously have provided good results, leaving aside the analysis of many of the existing alternatives. (Consumer, 2007, page 388).

2.6.3 psychoanalytic Theory :

The behavior of people is guided in an essential way by a series of deeper reasons of the human spirit and, therefore, difficult to understand for a analysis of logical to physical. These so-called ghosts that guide the behavior of the people, without them accept it in an open way, they are basically the sexual impulse and the aggressive impulse.

The majority of the actions of individuals are oriented to satisfy needs of sexual order, but as the society prevents the open demonstration of these tendencies, manifest in a hidden way through the behavior every day. (Consumer,

2007) For example, the use of tie in for men (garment completely unnecessary and up annoying, but very popular) would be driven by the symbology highly sexual of this garment (symbol phallic according to the psychoanalysts). Smoking might be a reminiscent of the activity of suction that all we do when we are babies, and who seeks, thus, to be carried out without motivating the reproach social practice would be used against individuals." (Consumer, 2007) On the commercial front, a multitude of products appear to be strongly linked to guidelines of a sexual nature of consumers.

The case of the cosmetics and the fashion female is for sure one of the most remarkable, resulting evident that products such as lipstick, the brassieres, high-heeled shoes, etc. Essentially seek to put in evidence specific elements of attraction sexual users. (Consumer, 2007) Moreover, the social resistance to accept this fact generates situations contradictory, as the women to use provocative clothing for men the watch, but get upset when they do. The male shaving is also a sample of these conflicts, as men they shave to be more attractive, however, are unable to recognize consciously, that is the reason of this behavior (assigning as a reason it-based considerations, the hygiene or the usual). (Consumer, 2007).

2.6.4 sociological Theory:

The main reason that guides the behavior of people in need of integration in their social group.

So many people are going to have behaviors of little or no background in economic or psychological behaviors they are intended primarily to be good to others. (Consumer, 2007, p. 390) The clearest example of this situation seems to be the fashion phenomenon, for in she observed behaviors inexplicable in the light of previous theories.

Chapter three: Advertising in function of neuromarketing.

Neuromarketing is governed by basic concepts of general of the Neuromarketing, types of advertising, functions, objectives and strategies of the same, is develops the analysis and study of how the brain works to the advertising, the types of Neuroinsights and conditioning the behavior of the consumer and the advertising sensory, the knowledge acquired in the same will comply with the objectives.

3.1 Neuromarketing:

Neuromarketing is the application of the techniques of neuroscience to marketing. Your goal is to get to know and understand the levels of care they show to the people different stimuli. In this way it tries to explain the behavior of the people from the base of your neural activity.

Is generated from the field of marketing, analyzing which are the levels emotion, attention, and memory that have different perceived stimuli of consciously or subconsciously, with the intention of improving the management of resources companies without increasing costs unnecessarily and increase the products there are on the market, thus improving the social well-being and understand the decision-making of the consumer. (White, 2010, page 9).

Neuromarketing studies the workings of the brain in the decisions of purchase. To do this examines, by means of the neuroscience, the way in which the stimuli advertising and brand impact on the brain's response. According to the specialists in Neuromarketing, the decisions of the consumers have as an anchor of the subjective feelings that are linked to sensory stimuli. (White, Neuromarketing, 2013) These, they say, are activated at the point of consumption below the levels of consciousness. For this reason, sometimes are useless market research, as analyze the levels-conscious consumers. (White, Neuromarketing, 2013).

3.2 Advertising:

Advertising is a form of communication that attempts to increase the consumption of a product or service, to insert a new brand or product in the market consumption, improves the image of a brand or reposition (or keep using the remembrance) a product in the mind of a consumer. This is done through advertising campaigns that spread in the means of communication in accordance with a plan of communication preset. (Eguizabal, 2008).

Advertising is the set of strategies that a company gives to know their products to the society. The advertising used as the primary tool the media of communication, these are so different and have so much expansion and impact on the public in general, and which are fundamental to the trade in general. If a product is not advertised, hardly people know him and are mean to him as something of good quality with regard to the name that it has. Advertising is a marketing strategy to position products in the global market, its participation in the expansion of the companies is accurate and necessary. (P., 2011).

3.3 Neuromarketing on role of advertising:

Neuromarketing is consolidated as one of the most profitable investments and efficient since it is through the brain research that identifies needs and interest of great informative value for brands. (Publicity, 2015) Neuroscience is a discipline that encompasses many sciences, including the advertising; which is concerned with studying the structure and operation of the system brain and nervous.

It is the base on which it is based the so-called "Neuromarketing". (Publicity, 2015) It is called Neuromarketing to the application of the research of the neuroscience on the market, in relation to emotion, attention, and memory. The goal of Neuromarketing is to understand better the relationships of consumers to make get messages to your subconscious that have a greater impact. Advances in the brain scan, magnetic resonance imaging, have been extraordinary.

At the time that an advertisement is displayed on our retina some areas of the brain are activated more intensely, however, is a condition inherent to the human being, but not because of an ad record a footprint in the brain, will be enough to buy compulsively the product that is offered to us. (Publicity, 2015).

It is confirmed in this way that advertising and marketing are eminently emotional and while consumers believe that the campaigns and strategies implemented launched by the brands respond to surveys and analysis, fully rational, so true is that the emotions that guide and accompany consumers in their decision buying, which has led the brand to go to techniques such as Neuromarketing to identify that demand in the brain of the consumer. (Discussing the decision of buying, 2011).

3.4 interactive advertising, persuasion, and consumption:

Advertising is a field that has always moved large amounts of money and that has conditioned patterns of behavior, habits and attitudes of consumers in general. Interactive advertising has been revealed, within our society, as a step necessary and unavoidable in order to adapt to the new expectations and needs of the digital age. (Inteco, 2009).

We have to mention any of the requirements, for the interactive advertising, and to his accessibility, represents the semantic web, or also called web 3.0. Thus, when constructs an advertising message which will be broadcast through a digital technology advanced, the coding of such a message can include information not present simple view. (Inteco, 2012).

The semantics, according to its creators, is in charge of defining the meaning of the words and in the case of the web 3.0 refers to the fact that web content can be a carrier of additional significance that goes beyond the meaning of its own textual said content. (Inteco, 2012).

The most important features of the interactive marketing campaigns aimed at the young people and with which they feel best represented, most identified are: to

Emotionality.

It is a resource that works well among young people, since they value the advertising that appeals to their feelings and emotions. An emotionality that adopts a new orientation, the more critical, which shows young people as they are, with their shortcomings, insecurities, flaws and boundaries in your personal and social life. b. Simplicity.: A trait that takes on a new meaning, since it is not appreciated only from a creative perspective, but he tries to be the expression of a moral attitude in front of a times of crisis, political uncertainty and social.

c. Realism:

The real world of the young is incorporated into the own story, in such a way that the young highly valued by the advertising that reflects as a collective, complex, not it is exclusive, that shows them handsome or ugly, careless, or solidarity, but of a realistic way.

3.5 Functions of advertising:

Advertising is conformed by 5 functions, which are:

3.5.1 informative Function:

We know that your purpose is to raise awareness of a product, and it applies not only to the image but also to the text or word. We know that the most important thing to give opening, launch or switch to image of a product it is essential to get to know through media, radio, television, or written and propagate that product or service. (Clow K. and.) As this feature has led to successful launches of these products aimed at a specific market segment. Likewise conveys information, attitudes and states of mind that are spread through it, provides information and persuades advertising. (Clow K. and.)

3.5.2 Function persuasive:

Not only you need to promote and inform if you do not also need to persuade, to convince, to for what it is worth all types of arguments. Here comes into play to promote and raise awareness of the benefits of the product, as well as also innovate strategies that boost the demand of this. Informs us based methods, psychological theories, social or cognitive. This can be used arguments rational approaches to emotional or be a hybrid of both. The persuasive strategy in advertising is in the emotions of the shaft motivational it flipped the attention, perfection and consumer behavior. (Clow K. and.) The message that is persuasive is to demonstrate the idea of the message of a focused textual or verbal and therefore not in the pictures or photos as other types of advertisements. (Clow K. and.)

3.5.3 economic Function. As a company needs to be profitable, how? Creating new needs, creating new consumers. Advertising is one of the great engines of the economy because our society is to a large extent, a society of consumer goods and companies need to know those products that do not think about hiring tremendous investment in advertising that ultimately ends up paying the consumer in the increase the value of the product. (Laza, p. 130) With this we come to the planning of state that, in order to achieve the goals proposed by the company in terms of sales, an investment need if you skimp on the cost of the propaganda you have.

To be able to get good results you have to invest a lot of time and capital and of this form to carry out such advertising to the consumer can be identified with this. (Laza, p. 130).

3.6 Objectives of advertising in the market:

Below are highlights of the main objectives of advertising:

3.6.1 general Objectives of the advertising:

Are three objectives, which are:

1. Report This is a goal it plans to achieve in the pioneer stage of a category products, in which the objective is to build primary demand. For example, manufacturers DVD had to inform in the beginning to consumers which were the benefits of your technology. (Essential concepts, P. Kloter, p. 282)

2-to Persuade. This objective is planned in the stage competition, in which the objective is to create demand selective for a specific brand. (Essential concepts, P. Kloter, p. 282)

3- Remember. This objective is applicable when you have mature products. For example, the ads of Coca-Cola have the prime intention of reminding people to buy Coca-Cola. (Essential concepts, P. Kloter, p. 282) .

3.6.2 specific Objectives of the advertising:

The objectives of advertising are much more specific. Stanton, Etzel and Walker, authors of the book "fundamentals of Marketing". Proposed following objectives:

1. Back to sales personal. The objective is to facilitate the work of the sales force giving to meet the customers

potential the company and the products that have the sellers.

2. Improving relations with distributors. The goal is to cater to the wholesale to supporting them with advertising.

3. To introduce a new product. The objective is to inform consumers about new products or of the line extensions.

4. Expand the use of a product. The target can be any of the following:
    - extend the season of a product,
    - increase the frequency of replacement
    - increase the variety of uses of the product.

5. To counteract the replacement. The goal is to strengthen the decisions of the current customers and reduce the likelihood of opt for other brands. (Stanton, 2004, page 625).

3.7 Types of advertising (first part):

The different types of advertising are the result of one or more classifications help determine the scope of the advertising, the different uses that you can give, the situations in which you may be used and the sponsors that can be used to achieve their goals. Therefore, it is very convenient that both advertisers and marketers know what are the different types of advertising and which consists of every one of them, which, give them a clearer idea about how, when and where to use this important promotion tool. (Clow, Advertising and Promotion, and Communication) Olguin, Allen and Semenik (1999). Provide a classification, which, in the opinion of the authors, is very useful for understanding the scope and the types of advertising, and is divided according to:

Is that the advertiser tries to create demand for a product category in general. In its pure form, the purpose of this type of advertising is to educate potential buyers as to the fundamental values of the type of product, in instead of mentioning a specific brand within the product category. (Richard, 1999).

Provide a classification, which, in the opinion of the authors, is very useful for understanding the scope and the types of advertising, and is divided according to:

3.7.1 Stimulation of the primary demand:

Is that the advertiser tries to create demand for a product category in general? In its pure form, the purpose of this type of advertising is to educate potential buyers as to the fundamental values of the type of product, in instead of mentioning a specific brand within the product category. (Richard, 1999).

3.7.2 Stimulation of the demand selective:
Its purpose is to point out the particular benefits of a brand in comparison with the of the competition.

3.7.3 Advertising response directly:
It is a type of advertising that asks the receiver of the message to act immediately. By example, the ads on tv that try to encourage recipients to to buy a particular product at a special price or using a good discount only last until midnight. (Richard, 1999).

3.7.4 Advertising response delayed:
Instead of searching for the stimulus of the immediate action of the public, advertising response delayed seeks to create the recognition and approval of a brand over time. In general, the advertising response is delayed is to generate the knowledge of the brand, strengthens the benefits of its use, and establishes a general taste by the brand. (Richard, 1999, p. 19-22).

3.7.5 Advertising business:

It is not designed to promote a specific brand, but that works to establish a favorable attitude toward a company as a whole, for example, Xerox and IBM. (Publicity, O'guinn, Allen, Chris, and Semenik, Richard, International Thomson Publishers, 1999, pp. 19-22.).

3.8 Types of advertising:

(Second part) Stanton, Etzel and Walker (2004). Provide a classification that, at the discretion of the authors, it is very useful for understanding the scope and the types of advertising, and is divided according to:

3.8.1 target audience:

Consumers or businesses: an advertisement is directed both to consumers or companies; well, it is an advertisement of consumption or advertisement of business-to-business.

3.8.2 The type of demand:

primary or selective. The advertising of primary demand is designed to stimulate demand for a generic category of a product such as coffee, electricity, linen or cotton. In contrast, the advertising demand selective aims **to stimulate demand for brands specified. (Stanton, p. 625).**

3.8.3 The message:

products or institutional. All of the targeted advertising is classified as product or institutions. Advertising of products focuses on a product or brand.

It is subdivided into 3:

1. Advertising of direct action:

Is looking for a quick-response, for example, an ad in a magazine that takes a coupon that urges the reader to send it to you to request a free sample.

Advertising of indirect action: this is intended to spur the demand in a period extensive. Its purpose is to inform or remind consumers of the existence of the product and point out their benefits. (Stanton, 2004, page 622).

2. Advertising of indirect action:

It is intended to stimulate demand in an extended period. Its purpose is to inform or remind consumers of the existence of the product and to point out its benefits. (Stanton, 2004, page 622).

3. Source: commercial or social:

Although the focus here the attention in the commercial messages, the most valuable of this support is the commercial, in which a friend or relative reliable recommend a product. (Stanton, 2004, page 622, and 623).

3.9 Type of strategies advertising:

There are three types of advertising strategies, which are:

1. **Strategies comparative:**
   Try to show advantages of the brand versus the competition.
2. **The media Strategies:**

It is a global plan for the short, medium and long term, where they were studied and it is concluded that means are appropriate, the recommended times to advertise. It is intended to achieve the greatest benefit at the lowest cost, reaching the target group established.

The media of mass communication (such as periods, radio, television and internet) are the the main means through which you can carry messages to groups of people large and diverse.

The media offer to the freedom of expression organizations a vehicle essential to bring information to an audience that includes everyone from the public general orders making decisions in the Government. (Advertising and Promotion and Communication) A media strategy is a plan that guides the way in which your organization interacts with the media.

They help to ensure that your messages are uniform, organized and focused. Have a media strategy means that your organization will not be simply reactive, that is to say, visible in the media only when an event or circumstance requires your comments.

(Advertising and Promotion and Communication) With a social media strategy, you can build and manage deliberately your image public, and their relations with the media, so that whenever you want to launch a campaign or respond to a situation, you have a capital to take advantage of.

A social media strategy that is specific to a campaign it relates to their strategy of media general, and is a plan on how to interact with the media to bring your message to a targeted campaign. (Advertising and Promotion and Communication)

The media strategies for specific campaigns may be easier to put into practice if you already have established relationships with the media through her strategy of general media; however, this is not a condition.

This phase we find ourselves in the way of reaching the largest possible part of our target audience the greater the number of impacts and the cost of the hood. (Advertising and Promotion and Communication).

3.10 promotional Strategies:

Stand out through constant promotions and is quite aggressive. The most important elements that is included in the promotional strategy within an organization of commercial, industrial, or service are: Advertising, personal Selling Packaging, and sales promotion.

3.11 Affiliate Marketing:

Affiliate marketing, especially useful with the interactive advertising, is specializes in getting results for companies. Encompasses all those business relationships in which a merchant (online store or advertiser) promotes your services or products using ads and affiliate (typically a web page inserts those ads and promotions on their web pages. (Advertising and Promotion and Communication) EXAMPLE: *Platform entertainment of Coca-Cola.*

The strategy communication is based on the concept: you decide. To convey the benefits that it involves the use of the new web of Coca-Cola, incorporated elements: Emotional (you are free to introduce yourself as you want, you have a territory in which to display your sign's identity) and Rational (new friends, new challenges, game, prizes, high value).

The advertising strategy is based on the transgression (live as you wish, there is no orders), the challenge (and win or lose, make friends or enemies, depends on you) and the differentiation (defined your virtual identity in front of the rest of the community, mark your territory). (Advertising and Promotion and Communication).

The color conditions us to buy:

The color penetrates into the mind of the consumer and can be converted to a direct stimulus for sale". (Dupont, 2004) "The importance of color in advertising is unquestionable. In the ads make patent the effects of functional, emotional, and aesthetic colors. These impress, to attract attention and express the result in a meaning and emotion.", But also communicate, as they have a value of sign." (Dupont, 2004).

3.12 Five ways to turn the advertising persuasion:

According to the web Portal, direct Marketing, in all advertising campaigns, there are persuasive elements that can be constructed using many different techniques, some of them very subtle, others are more direct.

Listed below are the main techniques of persuasion used by the ads:

(1) The beauty and the sex:

of the techniques of persuasion used by most advertising is the association of a product or an idea using the beauty or sexuality.

Sex is an undeniable "hook" to catch the consumer. Similarly, ads that convince the client of the effect "bezel" of a particular product.

(Clow, 2010, page 157) There are many examples of this means of persuasion, here is one in particular:

Figure N. 7 advertising soap Palmolive:

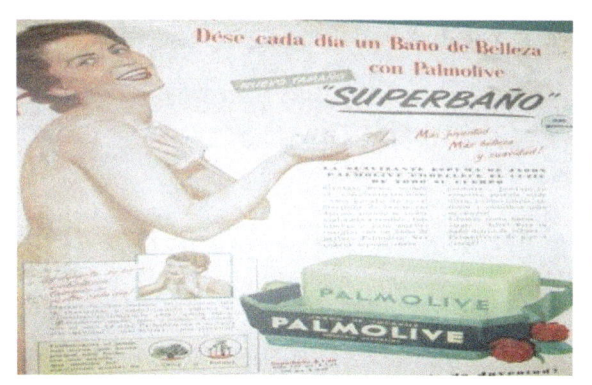

Source :
http://es.wikipedia.org/wiki/Sexo_en_la_publicidad

It shows a model in a pose exhibitionist, looking directly to the public, giving back, it seems to take a step towards the bottom of the ad, such as inviting customers to follow her.

This advertising shows that the implementation of sex and beauty in advertisements, it is not for nothing new, on the contrary, it is a marketing technique that has been under way for several decades. (Clow, 2010, page 157).

2) The affinity

consumers are willing to buy products which feel a certain affinity. This affinity can be constructed in several ways, for example, by associating a product with certain family values, or selling it exclusively to certain "elites".

The goal is that consumers feel that the product promoted is created in his image and likeness.

A clear example of this is are the advertisements for Coca-Cola, which is always characterized by partnering with the family and happiness, values that can make many people feel identified. (Clow, 2010).

"Merry christmas...take a coke".

A gas that is not specifically recommended for the health of children, it is associated with intangible values such as the family and the happiness, to accomplish any way to counteract this defect.

3) persuasion indirect

persuasion indirectly creates an association between a situation and a product, where in reality there is not.

An ad for a laundry detergent you can, for example, do you believe the consumer that the use of the detergent will have a beneficial effect on his life, family.

However, there is a direct connection between the family life and the use of a particular laundry detergent. It uses the relationship between a mother and son to promote the laundry detergent, which, although does not have any influence on the family life of the people, the advertising picture with the order that individuals make that connection easily, by themselves,
And in an unconscious way. (Clow, 2010, page 25).

4) The testimonies
of The testimonies of celebrities and consumers are used in advertising to arouse your customer's attention and make your time your confidence and trust.

When a person "common" ensures that a certain product has value, it generates in the audience a sense of credibility to that product. (Clow, 2010, page 185).

5) The information
The information, whether in the form of facts, figures or statistics, are used in advertising to convince the consumer of the credibility of the product promoted.

In some cases, it has real value, but in others, it is just a statistic "convenient" for the purposes of advertising. (Clow, 2010, page 188).

In some cases, it has real value, but in others, it is just a statistic "convenient" for the purposes of advertising. (Clow, 2010, page 188).

3.13 The four "P":

As we have already said above, once the persuasion of the consumer, by means of any of the advertising techniques mentioned in the previous point, a good way to ensure that the individual happens to be a "casual consumer" a customer of the brand, it is by means of the application of the marketing mix.

(Clow, 2010) The same is formed by a series of individual initiatives, on the whole, become the "weapon" that every entrepreneur needs to convert to a consumer's liability to a client. (Clow, 2010)

once this is achieved, the work will be to convert that customer in "partner", on client frequent.

These "weapons" they can be summarized in four main aspects to the time of capturing a customer, that was set in the years around 1960, Jerome McCarthy:

1) The packaging, is the presentation of the product, you must demonstrate all the qualities that this offers all of the benefits that you can get to give to the consumer whether to purchase it. The individual must "buy" the product just by looking at it, because you will find the solutions, you're looking for at first sight.

2) The price, is the key to position itself in the distribution, but it will depend purely and exclusively of the strategy you want to follow the company that offers the product or service. (Clow, 2010) unlike the other elements of the so-called marketing mix, is the Neuromarketing: the "cerebration" of advertising is unique in that it generates income, as the others mean a cost to the entity. The company shall fix the same by taking into account different aspects, such as:

a - Costs of production and distribution;
b-The margin that you want to obtain;
c- The competition;
d- The marketing strategies adopted; and - The objectives set out, among others.

3) The advertising, it should display the message you want to broadcast. Depending on what you want to market, will be the "vehicle" to present the product.

The relevance of this variable is to define what type of advertising is going to develop in function of the segment of consumers to which it is pointing. It is of vital importance to decide if what we want is that the brand is quickly known, positioned one way or the other, or if you are looking for is basically to sell more, in the shortest possible time. (Clow, 2010).

4) The distribution:

is based on the location of the product in the right place. It is comprised of four elements that shape the policies of distribution:

a) distribution Channels: or agents, involved in the process of moving the product from the supplier to the consumer.
b) distribution Planning: it involves decision making in terms of the logistics of getting the products to the consumers, and the agents involved, retailers or wholesalers.
c) physical Distribution: ways of transporting the product, stock levels, stores, location of plants.
d) Merchandising: techniques and actions that are carried out at the

point of sale. Basically, it consists in the presentation of the product in the store, as well as the advertising and promotion at the point of sale. (Clow, 2010).

"The transformation of the consumer in the customer" is a process long and arduous, but today, thanks to techniques such as Neuromarketing, you can become a process simpler and more predictable.
more simple and predictable. With the study of the human brain can "persuade" more easily to the consumer, because we know their desires, their preferences, and mainly their needs.

A time persuaded to buy for the first time the product or use for the first time, the service, the greatest challenge will be to transform it into habitual consumer. (Clow, 2010).
Here is where the need arises to apply the marketing mix, offering a presentation of the product that

meets the expectations of the customer, a price that is reasonable, without neglecting one of the most important features of a product, as is the quality, and taking into account the sector of the population to which it is pointing.

Advertising is another aspect that we cannot let go of, because when the consumer acquires for the first time, the product, the same should be transformed into the "vehicle" to which the product becomes known, and once that was purchased, the advertising should be the means to continue to persuade the consumer that the election is taken from the beginning was the most appropriate. (Clow, 2010)

Finally, the distribution of the product will play a dominant role, because if for]example, you want to introduce a product with a price above the average, in terms of products of similar characteristics, in a sector of the population with scarce resources, it will be an almost impossible task. We can conclude that to produce the "transformation of the consumer customer", we can't stop "listening" to the needs of the consumer. (Clow, 2010)

3.14 Advertising on the internet:

Since the beginning of the 1990s, the budgets for advertising on the internet have increased steadily.
 The funds for the advertising on the internet have a larger share of the total budgets of advertising and marketing.
 Many marketing experts believe that it is a very effective method to reach the 66 modern consumer, in particular the youth market, more

knowledgeable of the internet. (Clow, 2010, page 253)

3.15 Forms of advertising on the internet:

Have emerged four different categories of internet advertising. The first use was the banner ad or popup. Usually used in a graphical format. The second is the classified ad, which constitutes 17 percent of the online advertising budgets. The third and most important category of spending on internet advertising is the ads in search engines. These are the text ads that appear at the side of the search results when you enter specific words.

The last category is that of ads in media, and video. Is the category of more high-growth? This growth increase as the mobile phones and other devices that move forward hand in hand to the technology. (Clow, 2010, page 253)

3.16 internet and social Networks:

Social networks have become very popular among businesses and individuals that are trying to communicate with consumers.

The most famous sites are Facebook, Instagram and twitter.

These sites allow businesses to place ads and direct them to the interests, habits, and friends of the members, based on their profiles.

Brands such as Calvin Klein, Nike, Adidas, victoria's Secret and Ralph Lauren have a growing presence on sites such as YouTube. These types of sites allow companies to post videos, ads and other marketing materials. People can choose the videos that you want to see and share with your friends. (Clow, 2010, page 255)

3.17 e-Mail:

Another aspect of the strategy, interactive marketing of the company is to use with efficiency the e-mail. To be successful, a program of e-mail marketing must:

   1- integrate with other marketing channels

   2- based on web analysis

   3-combined with future monitoring systems for the web. (Clow, 2010, page 258)

3.18 web Analysis:

Is the process of analyzing that made consumers into the brand's website and other sites visited This analysis allows the company to create campaigns e-mail that provide the greatest likelihood of response. The growing use of the internet both by consumers and by companies has led many marketing teams to develop a website or presence on the internet. The key is to identify the functions that the web site you must play.

The main functions of marketing that play different websites include: advertising, support, sales, customer service, public relations, and commerce - mail. (Clow, 2010, page 258)

Conclusions:

In this research we evaluated the influence of Neuromarketing through advertising, which has become very important, in which neuroscience is one of the tools most commonly used in marketing to determine the consumer behavior today.

We learned about the concepts and overview of neuromarketing applied to the field of strategic consumer behavior, after the study of the mind, of the same allowing the marketers understand and predict the habits of the consumer in the market.

We determine the behavior of the consumer through the techniques and strategies used neuromarketing to capture the attention of the consumer constituting the methodology used to study the behavior of the same; where we can assert the knowledge of this science, that is to say invest in the emotions and feelings of the consumer, by means of something as simple as, providing them with a comfortable space and comfortable at the time of the purchase, which is performed at all stages of the process of consumption: before, during and after the purchase. It can be inferred that when developing an advertising strategy should take into account each one of the procedures that make it up, organizing way objective and precise combination of the necessary tools.

This will allow us to develop effectively in the competitive market and establish better communication with the market to which you want to transmit the message.

Finally, it is worth to mention the satisfaction achieved in terms of the goals for us are raised with respect to the subject matter addressed, waiting for it to serve as element of study and consultation to the students and people interested in a subject that is virtually new, and with very little material to deepen their study.

Bibliography:

White, H. M. (2010). Neuromarketing, . In H. M. White, Neuromarketing as a tool poderoza (p. 9).

White, H. M. (2013). Neuromarketing. In H. M. White, Neuromarketing (p. 9).

White, H. M. (s. f.). Neuromarketing. In H. M. White, Neuromarketing (p. 9).

Braidot. (2013). Neuromarketing. In Braidot, Neuromarketing (p. 24). Braidot. (2013). Neuromarketing in action. In Braidot, Neuromarketing in action (p. 15). Cayuela, O. R. (s. f.). neuromarketing. In O. A.

Cayuela, cerebrando business and services (p. 171). 1st edition.

Clow, K. E. (2010). Published, promotion and communication. In K. E. Clow, published, promotion and communication (page 472). Mexico.

Clow, K. Y. (s. f.). Advertising and Promotion and Communication. In K. Y. CLOW, Advertising and Promotion and Communication (page 472). Fourth edition. Consumer. (2007). Consumer behavior. In Consumer, Behavior of the Consumer (p. 387).

Cremades. (2014). Advertising. In Cremades, Advertising (p. 303). Diaz, P. (2012). Consumer behavior. In P. Diaz, the

Behavior of the Consumer (p. 321). Dupont, L. (2004). influence of advertising.

In L. Dupont, influence of the published. E., P. (2015).

Advertising. In P. E., Advertising. Echaberri. (2014). Neuromarketing. In Echaberri, Neuromarketing (pp. 28-29). Eguizabal, R. (2008). Advertising. In R. Eguizabal, Advertising. 70 Kanuk, L. S. (2010). the behavior of the consumer. changes and challenges. In L. S. Kanuk, consumer behavior. changes and challenges (page 560). mexico: Pearson Educacion. mexico. Kanunk. (2010).

The behavior of the consumer. In Kanunk, the behavior of The consumer (p. 309). Kennethe, C. Y. (s. f.). Advertising and promotion and communication. In C. Y. Kennethe, Publicity and promotion and communication (page 472). fourth edition.

Laborda. (2015). Neuromarketing. In Laborda, Neuromarketing (p. 209). Laza, A. (s. f.). advertising in the neuromarketing.

In A. Laza, advertising in the neuromarketing (p. 130). Marketing, d. (s. f.). Essential concepts, P. Kloter. In P. Hall, Concepts essential, of P, Kloter.

Neuromarketing. (September 26, 2019). encefalografia. Obtained from encephalographic:

https://www.google.com/search?hs=0ZG&sxsrf=ACYBGNR qpBHgmEFPfORn4V Qoqg5lcT1iEA:1576193705819&q=images+of+encephalogram &tbm=isch&sou rce=univ&client=opera&sa=X&ved=2ahUKEwivsrqPo7HmA hWizVkKHXRGB3kq sAR6BAgIEAE&biw=1306&bih=604#imgrc=QriHcsqZ21XVB

M: Neuromarketing. (05 10 2019). Magneto+Electroencephalography+pictures&client. Obtained of Magneto+Electroencephalography+pictures&client: https://www.google.com/search?q=Magneto+Electroencephalography+pictures&client=or pear&hs=31P&sxsrf=ACYBGNRKWwgkxivrq1hQTGvq2T9cFGVrjg:1570669240764&source=lnms&tbm=isch&sa=X&ved=0ahUKEwiS1Z7xvpDlAhWEmOAKHXGdDJsQ_AUIESgB&biw=1306&bih=604#imgrc=_-zCLmSt8oiq5M: Neuromarketing, P. and. (2011). Analyzing the decision of purchase. In P. and. Neuromarketing, Advertising, and Neuromarketing. P., G. (2011).

 Advertising and Promotion. In G. P., Publicity and Promotion (page 472). 71 Ramos. (2015). Neuromarketing. In Ramos, Neuromarketing (p. 303).

 Challenge pepci. (s. f.). Obtained from challenge pepci: http://www.dis.uia.mx/profesores/alex/tct/p2000/mariana/refresco7.html Richard, A. C. (1999). Advertising O'guinn. In A. C. Richard, Advertising O'guinn (p. 19-22). International Thomson. Salomon. (2010). Consumer behavior.

 In M. Salomon, Behavior of the Consumer (page 672). Schiffman. (2005). Consumer behavior. In Schiffman, Behavior of the Comsumidor (page 688). Mexico: Eighth Edition. Stanton, E. and. (2004). Fundamentals of Marketing. In E. and. Stanton, Fundamentals of Marketing (page 625). 13th ediccion. Zoega. (2015). Neuromarketing. In Zoega, Neuromarketing (p. 57). Zoega. (2016). Neuromarketing. In Zoega, Neuromarketing (p. 59). Marketing, d. (s. f.). Essential concepts, P. Kloter. In P. Hall, Concepts essential, of P, Kloter.

Neuromarketing, P. and. (2011). Analyzing the decision of purchase. In P. and. Neuromarketing, Advertising, and Neuromarketing. P., G. (2011). Advertising and Promotion. In G. P., Publicity and Promotion (page 472). Ramos. (2015). Neuromarketing. In Ramos, Neuromarketing (p. 303).

Annexes:

Which of the two draws your attention?

Annex 1; Own creation.

Easy like more: The brain is governed by basic shapes. Confusion is the same as rejection. The excess of elements generates confusion. The simpler the more you enjoy the brain and better assimilates.

Annex 2 Creating your own vision System low gender:

Women have a better overview (an ad with most elements, is better received by the female audience), while the men have a better view of tunnel (men prefer a few elements in an advertising that go with the grain). There is No advertising, unisex, or you are going more towards one side or the other.

Annex 3; Create own Search of tangibility:

The brain has a need to receive tangible things. The instinct for human biological required to possess, to touch, to feel. The symbolic element will land with the product. It is not the same to buy a software with cash to have it online or buy a plane ticket, get your hands on this ticket makes you already feel that these flying, tangible things are things that create feelings are very important, and these are things to keep in mind. Comforting to have the boxes of Windows instead of having the form online, in addition to look like Windows makes use of these rounded forms in their boxes.

Figure 4: Movistar Logo:

Source:http://community.movistar.is/t5/Welcome-and-News/Measures-taken-by Movistar-enrelaci%C3%B3n-to-the-SMS-Premium/td-p/379279

This example shows the use of the different companies do studies of Neuromarketing. In this case, was used for the logo design the impact of color, shapes, typography, etc. And this clearly shows the benefits that provides to the companies begin to think about how to get better for the consumer.

Printed in Great Britain
by Amazon